Praise for *What Every Child Needs to K*

GW00371849

Dr. Robert Manley's book "What Every Child
School: A Parent's Guide to the First 48 Months emp......
tance of the day to day interactions between child and parent that form a foundation for future learning. The daunting task of parenting is broken down year
by year with very helpful, concrete interactive tasks that develop patterns for successful learning in children. His emphasis on playfulness and responsiveness helps
parents understand that the ability to listen, to respect and to love the child is at
the core of shaping behavior. Teaching moments are more game like events than
disciplinary acts. Through the process of loving and listening, a parent shapes a
child's development of self- control, frustration tolerance, and respect and love for
learning. Technical and well researched, this book offers many practical examples
for parents that are not difficult to incorporate into daily experiences.

–Alida Schubert, PhD, Psychologist

This book about what every child needs to know before entering school provides
practical support for new parents who wish to develop resilient, responsible, kind,
curious and creative children. Dr. Manley projects a deep respect for thoughtful
parenting. His suggestions stem from his professional and personal experiences
with children, parents, and teachers during decades. Interestingly, at one point
he accurately contrasts authoritative and authoritarian approaches to parenting.
Importantly, he identifies all influential caregivers and their specific opportunities
to contribute to a child's healthy development. His guide should be a standard dis-
tribution in maternity wards, child care centers, and pre-schools. This handbook
should be read by all parents to be.

–Kevin N. McGuire, PhD, Director (Ret.),
New York State Center for School Leadership

The book entitled "What Every Child Needs to Know Before Entering School"
implies an expectation of a laundry list of facts and skills we might expect children to have before beginning their school-lives. Doctor Manley's deeper intent
opens windows into a child's world. His simple but thoughtful explanations of
themes like language acquisition and critical thinking are embedded in bilingual
and cross-cultural considerations of poverty, children's playtime and self-efficacy.
The themes he selects enable thoughtful and loving parents to envision how their
"mission" requires a combination of spirituality, love, and direction to nourish a
whole-child.

–Richard Bernato, EdD, Former Assistant Superintendent
for Instruction, Connetquot Public Schools, NY

WHAT EVERY CHILD NEEDS TO KNOW BEFORE ENTERING SCHOOL

A Parent's Guide to the First 48 Months

WHAT EVERY CHILD NEEDS TO KNOW BEFORE ENTERING SCHOOL

A Parent's Guide to the First 48 Months

Robert J. Manley, PhD

Illustrations by

Norah E. Manley

æon
ACADEMIC

Copyright © 2018 by Robert J. Manley, PhD

All rights reserved. No part of this publication may be reproduced, distributed, or transmitted in any form or by any means, including photocopying, recording, digital scanning, or other electronic or mechanical methods, without the prior written permission of the publisher, except in the case of brief quotations embodied in critical reviews and certain other noncommercial uses permitted by copyright law.

For permission requests, please address
Aeon Academic
7300 West Joy Road
Dexter, Michigan

Published 2018 by Aeon Academic
Printed in the United States of America

21 20 19 18   1 2 3 4

ISBN 978-1-943290-70-3
Library of Congress Control Number: 2018951455

Introduction

Linda, my daughter-in-law, inspired this book. When her neighbors elected her president of the PTA at her oldest son's and only daughter's elementary school in New Rochelle, New York, her new duties required her to bring guest speakers to the school. In addition to her work as a lawyer, she conducted meetings, devised school-wide activities with class mothers and the principal, and coordinated the PTA efforts to enhance the learning environment for the children.

When she needed a speaker at the PTA fall Parent Activity meeting, she called me and asked: "Bob, as a professor in the school of education and former superintendent of schools, would you give a brief presentation to our PTA on how children learn what they need to know before entering school?"

"Okay, Linda," I said, "I'll get back to you with a title in a couple of weeks." "Fine," she said, fully confident that I knew what I was doing. Neither she nor I knew how difficult it would be for me to condense my little warehouse of knowledge about children, how they learn, and what they need to learn before going to school into a thirty-minute presentation.

After much soul-searching and many conversations with parents raising young children, including another daughter-in-law, Barbara, who had been a financial analyst in New York City, I chose the selections that you will find in this book.

I assume that all parents can practice with their children good social behaviors and positive feelings associated with word games, readings, stories, and songs that every child should experience before entering school. Children need to learn how to ask a question and to offer a prediction to a story plot before going to school. When a child's answer is not what the story line reveals, parents can celebrate a child's new idea. They can offer their own insight that the author may be surprised to see the story turn this way too.

Parents prepare their children to be productive learners in a democracy by helping them acquire language and thinking skills from birth to age four. I realize many new parents have very little knowledge of the importance of the first forty-eight months in a child's life.

For young parents in the beginning of their marriage and career pursuits, parenting skills tend to be underdeveloped. High school students do not learn the most important parenting skills before they graduate. Too many parents raise children in an enterprise of trial and error. They raise their child with little knowledge of what helps children become lifelong learners.

Parents who face the stress of working and caring for young children have little time to read thick books about parenting skills with many references to field-based authorities. My daughters-in-law asked me to write a useful and informative short book. Barbara had this advice for me: "Try to help parents see what behaviors and attitudes are necessary for their child's success in school."

I believe new parents need to formulate an adult view of schools. Most parents have a cursory understanding of school based upon their experiences as children in school. Let's examine what schools and parents may encounter today.

At most schools, the curriculum is highly influenced by federal and state legislation, standards, and tests. Children and their needs have become secondary to the testing bureaucracy and the politically driven representatives who set public policy. Teachers, on the other hand, want children to be happy learners. Parents crave a child who is a happy learner. Not every child can be a happy learner in school, especially at the outset of school where freedom is limited and control of children's behavior is often the dominant theme.

The best schools have teachers who know how to manage a child's individual needs for freedom within the context of necessary cooperation that learning demands. New parents may have a difficult time with school cultures since most schools are not as responsive as Amazon.com.

Parents need a basic guide when dealing with school personnel. A workable guide is to approach all school personnel as professionals who are dedicated to their work and their students' well-being. Parents and teachers should be partners in the education of a child. At school, teachers have extensive authority and they have to take the lead in making parents partners.

Parents can facilitate this process by asking their child's teacher: "How can we help?"

Parents who approach principals and teachers in the same fashion they would approach their doctor or lawyer for professional advice enjoy valuable partnerships at their child's school. Parents who offer respect and trust to school personnel find school personnel are very responsive to their inquiries.

The school is not a ".com center." Parents are not purchasing a grade for their child. In schools, parents find that teachers have less freedom of choice than other professionals do at their work. Teachers have to adhere to federal and state mandates for testing, follow a grade-level curriculum, and address individual learning plans for many children simultaneously. Parents who seek to be partners with their child's teachers gain social and emotional capital with the professionals at the school.

School personnel and parents work well together when they agree about the social, emotional, and learning behaviors necessary for success in school. If any one of these three aspects of a child's healthy relationship with her or his school is unsatisfactory, parents, teachers, and other support staff should form a collaborative work group and help the child find successful learning and behavioral patterns.

Parents need to know how to prepare their child for lifelong learning. Parents can prepare a child for school at home long before the child enters her or his first classroom. Preparation for school is similar to being ready to join a play group. The ingredients are similar to preparation for the playground or a cousin's birthday party. Children have to learn how to share, to help, to listen, and to play a role in a group.

Most new parents want to know what matters to a child's sense of self-worth. They want their children to have self-confidence, determination, and the resilience to bounce back from disappointments and mistakes. Of course, they have to allow their child to fail to do something well for their child to learn how to overcome feelings of defeat. To enjoy the feelings attached to achieving success after practice and hard work, children have to learn how to overcome disappointments. Effective parents guide their children through difficult times. They model determination while trying to make something work in front of their one-year-old. They show disappointment when they lose a game or blocks fall down, and then, they try again.

Before writing this book, I bothered several new parents with questions about what they wanted for their children. Beyond the basic fact that they wanted children who cared about others and not just themselves, many desired children who would be able to read thoughtfully and calculate in meaningful ways. They wanted their children to become capable and caring young adults. They wanted their children to enjoy learning and sharing.

Some suggested very strongly that I present my story with a few succinct and important insights about the role of parents in their child's education. Several of these young parents stated: "Keep it simple and brief. We don't have time for dissertations on child rearing."

One of our sons, Michael, suggested, "Remember how a coach offers advice in the heat of a game. Give them the short version that includes pithy statements about the why, where, and how."

Our other son, Patrick, reminded me: "Parents worry about discipline, especially young parents. Older parents such as those in their late thirties do not seem to know how important discipline is. They do not understand that discipline is the art of self-control that leads to good character. Everyone wants to know how to raise a child who has good character, but few care about the aspects of self-discipline that are the foundations of character."

How Parents
Make a Difference

At my daughter-in-law Linda's invitation, after weeks of preparation, I found myself before an audience of parents who had come to learn what I knew about preparing children for school. When I finished my presentation, I answered several questions from the audience. As the session ended, my son Mike came over to me and said, "Dad, put this in a book. Keep it succinct so busy parents will read it. You have some good stuff here that you actually practice." Wow, my son thought I mostly practiced what I preached.

I suppose that is the height of compliments: an offspring who thinks you practice what you preach. In any case, when I told my other son and his wife about the encouragement I received, they thought I should focus a helpful book on parenting in the first forty-eight months of a child's life.

I decided I would write for the generation of parents who were raising their children in a global and digitized social world. Parents in this century live in a growing global economy awash with multicultural values and beliefs that clash with traditions. Art and music challenge conventions in a pervasive digital downpour. Social and interpersonal differences and religious, ethnic, and racial differences challenge shared civic beliefs and values. Personal identity struggles make the American culture dynamic, uncertain, and creative and at the same time contribute to anxiety and questions about self-worth. Parents bring many conflicting emotions to child-rearing, and one very important job new parents have is to clarify what they value and how they will treat their baby.

New parents should try to answer several simple questions. How will I control my own emotions with my child? How will I raise my child to be independent of me? How will I show my love for my child? How will I help my child to manage her or his emotions, fears, anger, and desires? How will I help my child appreciate reading? How will I help my child to use numbers to categorize things and to make responsible decisions? Parents can provide appropriate guidance with simple games such as presenting three small crackers in a dish to a two-year-old and asking, "How shall we share these crackers?" One answer might be to save one for Mommy and save one for Daddy and the child takes one.

The use of media to motivate a child and guide new learning is a big challenge currently.

In this media-driven world, how does a parent exert more influence on a child's personal identity than the pervasive imagery of commercial enterprises dedicated to profit from children and their parents? Is visual stimulation more important than personal identity?

How important is personal identity? In a recent study of adult orphans who achieved successful careers, Saundra Simonee (2013) found personal identity was the single most common attribute that these adults developed in childhood. In the case histories she studied of highly successful adult orphans, one or more adults helped these orphaned children to see themselves as good, kind, and caring persons who were able to learn. This positive vision of themselves belonged to each one of the successful orphans. They stated their greatest treasure was the belief in themselves as good people who could learn (Simonee 2013).

As I constructed this book, I tried to remember that language is imagery. Language connects thoughts and thoughts are a combination of sounds, feelings, perceptions, and words that attach to images in our minds and send emotions throughout our bodies. Those who teach language teach the mind to see, think, and feel.

Parents are the first teachers of language and should know that they are trying to teach their child to think as a good citizen would, i.e., as someone who helps others as well as oneself. This book is a guide for parents who wish to teach their child the language of self-discipline and its critical derivatives: words, numbers, time, calculation, decision-making, values, and virtue. Yes, the parent is the first teacher. Child-caregivers and other surrogate parents follow the first teacher.

Children become capable of self-regulated learning as young adults because of the adult support they receive from parents and other surrogates. No time with a parent is more important than the first forty-eight months when a child learns to communicate with language, to feel safe, loved, and able to give joy to others.

I hope this brief sojourn into the world of a child's early years is a pleasant and rewarding stroll for you. As you read these brief chapters, take the time to feel deeply how much you love each child in your life. Each child needs your support ever so desperately to develop into a confident and competent citizen. If this book helps you select what you will emphasize in your child's world, then I have accomplished what I hoped to do. The illustrations in this book represent a young artist's vision of what she saw in each chapter of this book. Enjoy her visualizations of parenting and let them be a window into your child's world too.

Finally, I want you to know that the many months I worked on this book and all the research that I did helped me to realize how much more I have to learn about the early life of children. I am sharing with you the little I know that will help your child be ready for school.

1

What Every Child Should Know by a First Birthday

The First Year

The first year of a child's life opens the human brain to the sounds of language. As a child suckles, a mother's words can be music to the mind. A father's voice may soothe the child's mind. The tone, inflection, and pleasantness of a parent's words convey warmth and love as a parent bathes, cuddles, and feeds a baby. Much of what the baby will become begins here at the touch of a parent. The sounds, rhythm, tone, and words that each parent shares daily with the baby lay the foundation for the future learning the child will do.

By the time children reach their fifth year, they should know how to recall facts from a story, an expository essay, a news story, a cartoon, a picture, a song, or a poem. Before beginning school, children should know how to answer questions about a story or an event, even one as simple as "What did this bear want?" They need to be able to summarize and formulate their own questions about stories, pictures, and songs (National Reading Panel 2000).

In order for these language skills to settle into the normal brain functions of a child, the first year of a child's life should include daily opportunities to hear, see, and feel stories, songs, poems, and tales of living events. To touch a story or an event, a child must feel the story or the event with his or her emotions. Facial and tonal expressions of parents and other adults who share stories with the child convey feelings.

An event can be as simple as a musical mobile, or the feel of a fingertip on the child's cheek accompanied by kind and loving words. Repetitive events, tones, poems, songs and stories, words, even sounds become the familiar patterns that infants recognize. The child's brain associates every experience with other sensory experiences and makes connections for future references.

In their book *Meaningful Differences in the Everyday Experience of Young American Children*, Betty Hart and Todd Risley point out that parenting is a combination of "language diversity, feedback tone, symbolic emphasis, guidance style and responsiveness" (1995, 159). They note that parents who provide large amounts of diverse language experience and encouragement to follow a sound or to touch an object have responsive children. They help their child learn to reach out and touch a hand or a toy. They attract the child's eyes to follow movement and sounds from a toy, for example, by shaking a bright rattle. Their children learn to observe parental movements and later become curious learners.

Parents of children who do well in school provide their own gifted environment at home. "They listen and prompt relative to what the child has to say more often than try to interest the child in adult concerns. They tend to encourage autonomy. They ask for compliance more often than they demand it. They tend to make language important. They name and explain everything that they encounter with their child" (Hart and Risley 1995, 158).

In the first year of your baby's life, if you ask me what you need to do, the simplest guide I can offer is "talk to your baby whenever the baby is with you. Tell your baby how you feel. Tell your baby about the weather every day. Relate a story about someone in the family in the morning, in the afternoon, and in the evening. Repeat these stories often in your baby's first two years."

Your stories about real people whom you love and who make you happy or sad are the foundations for the learning capacity you will build within your child. The tone you use with real stories about people, animals, and birds ring true to your child. Stories you read to them should have an adventurous tone of the unknown next page. Children enjoy changes in tone. Your voice is a musical instrument that your child loves to hear. Use your voice to soothe and comfort your child. You are your child's closest friend and protector in his or her first forty-eight months. Your child senses all of your feelings and dispositions. Give your child the support, encouragement, and love you would want if you were totally dependent on another larger person for all of your care.

2

Parent-Child Interactions
in the First Year

How does interaction with a child translate into meaningful activities on an individual scale of one child and a parent and of one family and the children? Parental language, feedback, and tone express attitudes toward the child as a learner. Parents' commentary and enthusiasm are directly associated with the vocabulary a child uses later. The rate of vocabulary growth a child demonstrates predicts later the general rate of knowledge acquisition that an IQ (intelligence quotient) score estimates.

Remember IQ scores are estimates of how quickly your child is learning compared to an ideal learning cycle. An IQ does not set a cap on what a child or an adult can learn. An IQ merely estimates a current rate of learning in terms of what learning should have taken place in the past among a normal sample of children at a specific and similar age. Do not place limits on your child's capacity to learn, especially if your benchmark is a standardized test score such as an IQ. Your child's capacity to learn is not determined by an IQ score. Measurements of intellectual achievement predict likely outcomes; they do not limit achievements.

The interactions between parent and child, surrogate parent and child, child caregiver and baby determine how many language patterns and words a child will acquire before school. Interactions with language attached to close human touch and visualizations determine how well the child will be able to use language. Children in typical middle-class homes experience a great deal of language interactions with their parents and adult caregivers. Every child benefits from high levels of language use that broadens the child's sense of word meanings and how to sequence words.

Watching television is a passive event in which the human brain creates patterns of small dots and colors according to a preordained plan of the broadcaster. Frequently, the sounds and visuals of a television program lack the power of human touch. During the first forty-eight months of a child's life, human touch, warm voice tones, and loving facial expressions cultivate a healthy mind and spirit in a child. Television offers very infrequent knowledge creation and active learning for a child. Watching television is a passive activity devoid of sound emotional exchanges that a child and a parent can create. To learn, children need to engage, to touch and feel their environment as well as share their environment with other caring adults.

Children learn by crawling, exploring, and playing. Placing a toy close enough to a baby that the baby has to reach for it creates an interactive event for the baby. Babies learn to reach for a soft colorful toy at a very young age. As soon as a baby begins to crawl, parents can devise many hide-and-seek games with two pillows and a toy.

As the baby grows, more creative acts can be offered with blocks, toy cars, dolls, and stuffed animals. They can be organized by shapes, colors, and sizes. Babies are very observant and they will imitate what they observe as they become more mobile.

Rather than have a passive child watch movements on a television screen, parents can play games with toys, build a line of stuffed animals within the watchful eye of the baby, and tell stories with toys, stuffed animals, and even pieces of fruit. Parenting can be one of the most creative uses of the adult brain when parents think of themselves as their child's first teacher.

By one year of age, a child is an active learner. The more movement parents initiate in their child's daily activities, the greater the capacity the child will have to learn new skills later in life. Dancing to a rhythmic song in a parent's arms helps the child to follow and imitate dance steps, hand motions, and words in songs. These activities expand the child's capacity to recognize patterns. Such redundant physical acts enable the brain to develop the thinking skills to solve complex problems later in life.

Complex skills and understandings rely upon simple tasks repeated with ease. Diverse language patterns, used frequently with a child, enable complex and creative thinking that children do later in their growth cycle. Every interaction parents have with their child adds to their child's capacity to understand the world into which they have been born.

Parenting is an awesome gift. Choosing to foster a child is a profound act that one must commit to with a huge sense of responsibility. There is joy in the life-giving force one undertakes as a parent. Also, there are many sacrifices and worrisome nights that parenting a child brings. Only deep love and commitment to the baby's needs above all other needs ensure parenting will be done with the care a child deserves in the first twenty-four months.

First-Year Language Diversity Expands Thinking Skills

During the first thirty-six months of a child's life, language diversity relates strongly to a child's use of vocabulary with those who care for the child. "The more often a child hears words used in association with a variety of events and other words, the more varied and refined are the meanings of words for the child" (Hart and Risley 1995, 150).

Language diversity begins as soon as the mother encounters the child, in vitro too. Babies have a receptive language center in the brain that records patterns of human voice sounds. This receptive language center expands as poems or songs and other language-rich stories full of human feelings embrace the child's brain. Parents who read brief storybooks that involve human emotional content daily and nightly to a baby engage the receptive language center of the baby's brain and create patterns of recognition for future language learning. One of the stories we enjoy is Walt Disney's *Bambi* adapted by Melvin Shaw for Golden Books. The illustrations are beautiful and the story line, although simple, is filled with human emotion.

Parents who speak more than one language should think of reading books and singing songs in dual or multiple languages to their child. The baby's brain is open to multiple language patterns. Some multilingual parents dedicate parts of the day or the week to one language or the other. Children respond positively to consistent and constant reinforcements. Children master what they hear and see repeatedly. Remember, the natural growth of the child's response to diverse languages in the first thirty-six months indicates how open to multiple languages this child is. Dual-language enrichment should be consistent and regular for the child to accept it as a natural pattern. Children associate different languages with different people, times of the day, and activities such as eating. Dual-language parents may want to make breakfast or dinner one of the solitary-language experiences. Also, books in both languages should be read consistently if the child is to master the sequence of sounds, syllables, and words in each language.

Each child reacts differently to language stimuli. Some children are very receptive and yet, not ready to be active users of language in their first twenty-four months. Other children use words in sentences very early in their first thirty-six months. Parents should try to capture a child's attention when they speak, read, or share pictures in a storybook. After the second year of life, a child should be able to point to things in a book or in a room when asked questions such as: "Where is the blue ball?" or "Where is Bambi now?"

Children respond positively to consistent patterns of language usage at home. Each family that is capable of engaging a child in multiple languages should decide what days and times are best for each language. Children often speak the language of a grandparent at home, the language of school with parents if they know that language, and the language friends or family members like to use. To expand the child's knowledge of grammar or correct sentence structure in a language, parents can read small books to the child in the target languages.

A dual-language user has the advantage of seeing the world through multiple perspectives. For instance, one language may treat time as a measurement of distance while another language would treat the same event as a measurement of volume. In one language, a wedding lasting two hours might be called a "long wedding" while in another culture that wedding would be described as a "big wedding."

Many researchers note that vocabulary growth at age three relates strongly to the wealth of the parents. People confuse associations with causal events. Poverty or wealth will not in itself determine vocabulary growth. Hart and Risley (1995) found that a child's acquisition of new words was highly influenced by the lower use of words and stories and feedback from parents who were poor. In a home with high levels of poverty, many factors may contribute to the fewer number of words a child hears and the fewer stimulating exchanges between parents, caregivers, and child.

Parents who know the power of reading, singing, counting, and sharing creative stories with a child try to deliver those experiences as often as possible. Language usage, reading and comprehension skills, and thinking skills are associated with extensive vocabularies that children learn early in their development (Lesaux and Kieffer 2010).

Having less wealth does not reduce a baby's acquisition of new words nor does it alter the baby's word reproductive capabilities. How the parent and child caregiver use words delimits or expands the capacity of the baby to learn and to use language.

A child needs constant and consistent reinforcement of language and number systems. Each day in a child's life is a learning event. Each day can be rich in human development or devoid of human fun and play. A parent who sings, recites rhymes, reads poems, tells stories, and counts toys in different ways (e.g., based on size) presents his or her child with a gift of future learning capacity.

4

Poverty and Language Acquisition

Hart and Risley (1995) found that among hourly wage earners the amount of words directed at a child in a purposeful conversation differed significantly from family to family. They reported that parents and other child caregivers who were unemployed tended to use less language with their babies than mothers did in many families where the head of the household was an hourly or contract worker. Parents who were college graduates spoke many more words to their child than those who were not college graduates. In fact, in their research with new parents they found that in the first thirty-six months of the baby's life, the difference could be millions of fewer words addressed to a child born into a household with generational poverty.

Parents develop their child's brain with the simple, rarely complex, work they do with language, storytelling, and songs. All parents can tell stories by describing their surrounding environment, such as the morning, the weather, and the color and feel of things in the house or apartment. Every parent who knows the value of storytelling and songs can be highly communicative with her or his child.

Although family income serves as a predictor of academic performance across large populations, parents can influence the learning cycle by engaging in several simple activities with their child at home. If parents use the skills they have in storytelling, play, and song, they can enrich a baby's first twenty-four months without needing more money. As a twelve-year-old, I had to cut cardboard soles for my sneakers that were worn through the soles because my mother did not have three dollars for a new pair of Keds sneakers. I played in a championship basketball game with those sneakers. We did not have much beyond necessary expenditures for our apartment, food, and clothes. Language enrichment came from our mother reading to us and our father telling stories to us.

Feedback tone from a parent or caregiver can be positive or negative; it can encourage or discourage the child to use new words (Hart and Risley 1995). Parents can encourage a baby to use words by offering repetitions of words and extending words in forms as simple as the following pattern: "Mama," "Mama," "My Mama." Repetitive efforts with smiles and laughter from a parent that engage a child in mimicking word patterns enable the child to enjoy words and learning.

In the last quarter of their first year, babies begin to mimic sounds. Long before the ninth month after a child's birth, parents should be extending language usage in formations attached to actions. When a baby can sit on the floor, one may roll a ball to a child. A parent might say, "Ball, ball, roll the ball." "Big ball, big ball, roll the big ball." "Big, red ball. Big, red ball, roll the big, red ball."

Then, use a small, blue ball to do the same thing. Whatever the baby boy or girl shows an interest in, his or her eyes follow and can become a language development story. Parents who understand this premise of language pattern recognition can use any number of inventive patterns that they enjoy creating, for example: "car, big car and small car" and "doll or small doll and big doll."

Language games and actions extend language learning in young babies during the first year of life and make all toys and stuffed animals potential stories. All parents can devise their own games that they enjoy playing with their baby. The most important understanding that a parent should adopt is that playing word games with toys, colors, names, and numbers shapes the future capability their baby will have to learn new things.

When a child misses these enriched exchanges with a parent or daily caregiver, the child often exhibits delayed learning patterns in school. The school will have to extend the child's learning day by two to three hours to make up for the lack of learning in the baby's home during the first thirty-six months of the baby's life.

Children learn to understand and use symbols early in their development when they have the right stimulation. Symbolic emphasis "denotes the relative amount of a child's experience with language that refers to relations between things and events" (Hart and Risley 1995, 152). When parents name people and things, describe relations, and use the past tense or add adverbs and adjectives to sentences, they set the stage for a child to understand connections between people and among things and people.

Parents can relate stories to their child about simple experiences such as how Mom and baby went to the store, saw a big truck, watched clouds block sunlight, or listened to the rain fall. Parents have unlimited events and stories to retell to a child that will open a child's mind to words and thinking about things and how they happen.

The richness of a parent's imagination provides the wealth of knowledge children need to acquire language and thinking skills. Parents who have fun with their child have a child who has fun with them.

5

Parenting Style and the Use of Words in a Child's World

In the second twelve months of a child's life, word games and questions that elicit decisions expand the cognitive capacity of the child. Parents can create word games with simple photographs. For instance, if a mother has a photograph of her mother and her sister, she might point to each person in the photo and say: "Aunt Gail is my sister. She is tall. Grandma Joanne is my mother. She is short. I am taller than my mom is. Who is my mom? Who is the tallest, Aunt Gail, my mom, or me?" Photos of familiar people attract a child's attention in a similar way that the page of a child's storybook does.

If a parent looks at a photo with a child, poses an interesting question, and then points to the answer before stating the response, the child's brain becomes open for the response. After multiple practices of simple tasks, children point to the answer before the parent does and then, when they are ready, they say the answer.

In year two of a child's life, a word game can become a math game with any three items of different sizes. "If we have three cars or cups and they are different sizes, which one is the biggest? How many are smaller than the biggest one?" Numbers are part of language. They are a derivative of language and help us to describe the world we encounter. Numbers help us to make decisions. Parents can expand their child's world by helping the child to use numbers to count and to make decisions.

For instance, a parent can present four tennis balls to a child. She can give one to the child, put one in a shoebox, give another to the child, and give one to herself. She can count: Jillian has two balls. Look one and two. Mommy has one ball. How can Mommy have two balls? She can point to the shoebox and get that ball. She can count two sets of balls: one and two; one and two. She can give Jillian one of her balls and count Jillian's balls as one, two, and three. She can count her ball as one. She can ask: How can Mommy get another ball? She can look in the shoebox and say, "No more balls. Can Mommy have one of Jillian's balls?" Now when each of them has two balls, she can roll a ball to Jillian and Jillian can push a ball back to Mommy. A simple game of ball playing can become a game of number applications and lessons in sharing and being fair.

Parents teach culture beliefs and expectations in their stories about other important people in their child's life. Stories reinforce for their child the kinds of behavior that are good and those that are bad. Fairy tales always conveyed the cultural values of a people or a community. Family stories and many games can serve the same purpose.

The story *The Little Engine that Could*, in which the small engine tries to mount a mighty hill, repeating over and over again, "I think I can, I think I can," demonstrates the power of positive thinking that a child carries within her beliefs into adulthood.

For instance, when a mother's sister enters the room and the mother says to her baby, "Here's Aunt Gail. She is my sister. I love my sister. Aunt Gail will feed you your peaches," the mother is establishing a pattern of openness with her child. If this pattern repeats over again, week after week, with many members of the family and friends, the baby becomes open to new voices and people.

By the time the baby becomes an eleven-month-old child, she will have received an enriched language pattern that, as a three-year-old, she will use for future learning. She will be open to more people and more curious to know how people differ and how they are the same.

Young children have few limits on their potential to learn when they receive warm and loving encouragement. Children recognize very early in life the meaning of a parent's tone of voice. They know love, care, joy, delight, and their opposites. Raising a baby to be a responsive, warm, and curious four-year-old is a time-consuming and creative job. Children respond at different rates and they all require large amounts of patience and consistency.

Many new parents underestimate the complexity and dedication the parenting of a baby requires. It never is good enough to repeat the parenting and guidance style of one's own parents and caregivers. Your own child is unique and needs a personal touch based on who she or he is. A personal approach requires parents to be very observant and interactive with their child. Raising a child is not a traditional act in which one repeats what your parents did for you. A child is a one-time miracle bursting into this fourth dimension of time. Time and your attention is what the child will demand.

New parents need to decide before a child is born what parenting style they will use. They need to describe how they want to attend to and feel about their child. They need to decide how to express love for their child, how to share responsibility for the child, how to encourage their child to explore the environment, and how to set limits for the child.

Will a time-out rug or chair be the primary source of discipline for the two-year-old explorer who cannot keep away from the stove? How will we guide our two-year-old to comprehend and accept "no" as an answer is a question every set of parents needs to resolve.

Should a firm tone of "no" and a warm distraction become our primary practice? Will disciplinary actions include an explanation of why a "no" is the necessary response? Shall we commit to a patient, supportive, firm, and loving discipline approach to our child before the child crawls? Shall we select an ideal parenting style so that we will know how far we stray from the ideal as we deal with the day-to-day issues of raising a two-year-old? In other words, shall we try to predict how we should act and perform as a parent before we play that role?

If new parents sit together and describe to their partner how they would like to behave as a parent, they can support each other better and their child will benefit from the consistent love and guidance the parents offer. Children never benefit from parents divided against one another. When parents disagree about discipline or even allowable limits, they need to settle their disagreements in private and away from the child.

In the second year of life, a child presents a limitless capacity to learn. At the same time, they have an extraordinary need for adult guidance in order to feel safe and secure. Parents have to strike a balance among guidance, love, learning, and exploration. Striking the balance is like playing baseball, golf, or basketball. Each of these sports requires skills that players learn by making mistakes. Parenting demands consistent effort to learn how to do better each day.

As Derek Jeter stated on Mother's Day, May 14, 2017, when the Yankees retired his jersey number (2) and placed his plaque in Monument Park, "I just tried to play better every day." Effective parents take the same approach. They try to be better parents every day and one day, their child, having become an adult parent may say, "Thank you for always being there, never giving up on me, and working so hard to be a good parent."

6

Parenting Style Matters to a Child's Self-Image

All parents have a guidance style that they usually adopt from their own experience as children. For some parents, the only guidance style that they have known is one they learned at home and it may be negative, critical, and harmful. Hart and Risley (1995) note that a positive guidance style prompts a child to try something new. In the positive guidance style, parents ask the child to improve by offering encouragement such as "Can we try that again?" These effective parents avoid such statements as "That's wrong" or "That's no good."

Parents model the desired behavior and by doing so, imply a parent's confidence that the "child is motivated to improve and does not need to be ordered to do so" (Hart and Risley 1995, 153). Some parents ask, "Can we put our toys back in the box before lunch? Someone could trip on one of the cars. Help Mom put your cars in the box." In this scenario with a child beginning his or her second year, Mom or Dad can model the desired behavior and wait for the child to follow. Time together and sharing lunch is the reward for practicing good behavior.

Parents who use more guiding than demanding interactions with young children tend to have four-year-olds who use more words in appropriate ways to convey their thoughts. Some simple examples that give a baby the opportunity to make a good choice are questions that elicit a simple "yes" or "no" such as: "Can we dance?" "Can we dance to this music?" "Can we sing?" "Can Zachary sing?" "Shall we pick up our toys? "Shall we pick up our toys so we can have dinner?" "Can we say 'So big'?" "Can we raise our arms and say 'So big'?" Every action related to word patterns reinforces the language usage in the child's brain.

These simple sentences played out in multiple settings over and over again in the first two years of a baby's life by parents who want to guide rather than direct their child lead to higher levels of self-confidence as well as analytical and problem-solving skills in the child as a six-year-old and later as an adult.

Ira Gerald (2007) conducted a study of African American children in an urban elementary school in New York. He discovered that parents who avoided permissive parenting practices or harsh authoritarian ones and engaged in a more authoritative set of expectations that required their child to listen, explain, and be responsible and helpful, had children who performed at the proficient level on New York State reading examinations in fourth grade.

Hart and Risley (1995) and Gerald (2007) discovered that effective parenting is a style that one can learn through practice. Almost anyone who wishes to develop a child into a confident learner can choose an authoritative parenting style over a permissive or authoritarian style. The most important difference is that the authoritative parent seeks to develop the child and the authoritarian parent seeks to control the child as if the child were an object to be owned and operated by the parent. Authoritative parenting guides the child to be responsible, self-confident, and self-disciplined.

The most productive parenting behavior to select with an appropriate level of intensity and tone is one that responds to the child as he or she presents himself or herself at that moment. Hart and

Risley note, "Parent responses reflect a parent's interest in supporting and encouraging a child's practice and the parent's appreciation of, and adaptation to, the child's current skill level and choice of topic" (1995, 154).

At a recent dinner with friends who are new grandparents, we had the privilege of hosting their son and daughter-in-law and thirty-four-month-old grandchild. The child decided that she would like to hear my wife play the piano, and she took my wife's hand and led her to the old, upright piano we had. Later, in the evening, the child selected rubber dolls of the seven dwarfs from Disney's *Snow White*. She wanted to play a counting game. She lined the dolls up in a straight line, grabbed my hand, and moved me to the floor. She told me to count. As I counted one to seven, she repeated the numbers after me.

When we finished counting several times, we shared a "high five" handshake. Then, she decided she wanted bigger people to be the mother and father of the dwarfs. She gathered two large rabbits from the toy box, and when I asked her who they were, she said, "Mommy and Daddy." I asked a second time: "Who are those big people? She looked at me and said, "This one is their mommy and this one is their daddy."

Obviously, she has an enriched environment where her parents provide her with multiple responsive opportunities daily, at home and in her day care center. The parents' wealth did not create this responsive and creative child. Their actions and their language diversity, feedback tone, symbolic emphasis, guidance, and responsiveness enriched her home environment. All of these actions made the difference in the life of this not quite three-year-old.

What can new parents of any age and wealth do? They can learn the basic understandings that enrich a child's world. They can provide the appropriate level of engagement and support for a child's explorations and play. They can help their child to make decisions.

When a child listens to human communication, the child masters pattern recognitions and the intricacies of human communication.

Parents and care providers for young children should know that the frequency with which they use words and sentences to communicate with a child about fun and interesting topics influences the language skills that the child uses at school.

In the twenty-first century, many parents ask, "Is technology more important than song and storytelling?" Not every parent has the latest technology or the skill to regulate personal learning or even be effective in managing a child's use of technology. Most parents in the twenty-first century can access a smart phone and a book like this one or other helpful parenting guides. Access is not sufficient to develop knowledge or skills for parenting. Sensitivity, insight, and love for your child build as you come to know your child. You will need guidance as we all do as we engage in doing something we have never done before.

Several basic practices are very helpful in raising your child. Observe your child's behavior and note her or his feelings. Listen to your child. Converse with your child as you would with anyone else. Be sensitive to how your child feels. Respond to your child's feelings. Seek guidance from informed people about raising your child.

As a new parent, your child's pediatrician is a good source of guidance on nutrition for your baby, and on other health care and dispositional issues. You should schedule visits with your pediatrician to discuss how to develop the cognitive, social, and emotional well-being of your baby. Pediatricians and pediatric nurses have the training to be helpful to you. Actually, your local librarian who is trained in children's literature can offer significant guidance in each of these topics and any other questions you may have about raising your child.

There are websites that show digital experiences that incorporate sights and sounds to stimulate the child's brain. None of them have the warmth and love of a mother's touch and tone. They do not broadcast a father's kindness and encouragement. Digital experiences will not replace a song shared by a parent and child. Games, stories, imaginary events, pictures, and shared explorations in a park with a parent or grandparent are the joyful memories a child brings into adulthood. These memories verify the child's self-worth as an adult. Nothing is more valuable to a child's development than the feeling that "I am important to someone."

Remember, as a parent, your primary responsibility is to make it possible for your child to feel loved. A child senses if a parent has low or high expectations for good behavior, for learning, and for sharing. Parents create the early world of feelings in which the child lives and learns (Rotello 2003). It is an awesome gift to be the creator of your child's world for twenty-four months. As your child explores his or her environment, the world grows far beyond the limits a parent can control. For this reason, the values and sense of self parents help a child gain are the foundation upon which a child will build an adult life.

You are your child's first teacher. Be sensitive to what makes your child smile, laugh, express joy, or frown. Why does your child cry? Does he or she feel alone or unsafe? Is your child feeling discomfort, pain, or hunger? How can you comfort your child? These are very basic questions that parents encounter daily (Rotello 2003).

Effective parental responses always begin with a warm and loving touch, a cuddle, and soothing words. A clean diaper and/or breast milk or other sustenance may suffice. Sometimes, a child's condition requires great patience and loving care, and sometimes a crying child is reacting to an allergy. When in doubt, consult your pediatrician. Your loving voice is the best support you can give to your daughter or your son. Always have the courage to consult others with more training and experience when you feel you do not know what to do.

7

The Absolute Essential Experience

Just what should a baby hear from Mother, Father, and other caregivers in the first twenty-four months? Babies need to hear human voices, alive and full with emotional ranges of joy, sadness, love, kindness, surprise, determination, and even small amounts of disappointment when the baby spits out her baby food. Frustration and anger have tones of their own that parents must moderate and control. In small dosage and moderate tones, frustration and anger prepare children for the real world; in large dosage, they are harmful to the child's well-being.

Many emotions appear in children's stories such as *Goldilocks and the Three Bears* or *Jack and the Beanstalk* and other classics in children's literature. Almost all communities have local libraries with a librarian who is reachable by email or by phone for questions regarding what books to select for children of every age.

As a new parent, you may want to access this resourceful public servant and all she or he has to offer in the area of children's literature. Most community libraries have a librarian trained in the appropriate literature for children. Explore Caldecott Award–winning children's books online or at your library. Consult with your library's expert in children's literature at no charge by phone, email, or in person at your local library. Get to know your local children's librarian to find expert suggestions for literature to select for your child's language development.

Reading stories and playing games are comforting events that bring children and their parents closer. Children need parents close to them. They need loving adults to spend time with them. They need to hear adult voices change their tones and alter word patterns as their stories unveil kindness or selfishness, and other admirable or less desired behaviors within the tales they relate.

In a busy world where parents travel frequently for work, spend long hours at projects related to their jobs, or work more than one job, they have to rely on surrogate caregivers to use repetitive language events that their babies and young children enjoy.

Repetitive language attached to actions and visualizations in books prepares a child to use language independently at three years of age. Parents should select common storybooks that a caregiver, grandparent, aunt, or uncle might use to build language routines for their child. Familiar books, pictures, and stories build a baseline vocabulary when they are shared regularly with a child.

Songs are important learning tools for children too. Parents should share songs they like to sing with a caregiver. When a child hears familiar songs repeatedly, the child experiences constancy in language usage. When adults sing interesting and delightful songs or recite nursery rhymes, the child's mind masters the language patterns within the rhymes.

There are many children's books and songs or poems that convey enriched language, symbols, knowledge, and virtues that young children should learn. Each culture, religious practice, ethnicity, and race has an abundance of traditional stories and songs that children should hear often. Some parents believe their responsibility to educate their child can be handled with multimedia products.

Television and computer software can reinforce adult patterns of language that babies and young children developed previously with their parents and caregivers. By itself, television is no substitute for the responsive adult who engages a child in a game.

New mothers and fathers may want to know what stories to read, what poems to read, what songs to sing, what games to play. I do not want to give you a list because my list is restricted to my own cultural experiences, religious practices, and my history in the northeast of the United States and New York City where I was born and raised. What I will give to you are some prototypes that you may use as rubrics to select your own valuable language and rich experiences for your baby. (See the Appendix for other models.)

One of my favorite poems is a short one that I recite often to our little grandchildren to put them to sleep:

> Had I the heavens' embroidered cloths,
>
> Enwrought with golden and silver light,
>
> The blue and the dim and the dark cloths
>
> Of night and light and the half-light,
>
> I would spread the cloths under your feet:
>
> But I, being poor, have only my dreams;
>
> I have spread my dreams under your feet;
>
> Tread softly because you tread on my dreams.
>
> (William Butler Yeats, "He Wishes for the Cloths of Heaven," Collected Poems 59).

Two lovely stories that we read to our babies are: *The Little Engine that Could* and *You and Me, Little Bear*. Why did we select these stories? They were important to us because they taught values that we cherished. Both stories teach the value of hard work and determination. Both stories teach that personal responsibility is natural to life and so is a caring attitude toward others.

In addition to these two stories, we selected many others that hit a respondent chord in us. These stories we read frequently. Our children learned every word in these stories.

Some songs that we sing in a child's first twenty-four months have a pleasant rhythm like "Twinkle, Twinkle, Little Star" and

"Rock-a-Bye Baby." Other songs that we like have unique language patterns like "Hush, Little Baby" and "Happy Birthday." "Do-Re-Mi" from *The Sound of Music* is a favorite of ours too.

From the first day our baby was home, we began to sing the ABC alphabet song and a counting song that started with "One little, two little boys or girls." We were determined that our children would know their alphabet and their numbers one to ten by the end of their second year.

For the most part, they learned these sounds and symbols by rote memory in their first year and would take most of their second year to use them in a meaningful and thoughtful way. By the end of their second year, our babies had learned to select the first letter in the words *mom* or *dad* and the letters in their own name. The development of the skills for letter and sound recognition began as soon as we brought our babies home from the hospital when we began to sing the ABC song to them.

We prayed every night and gave thanks to God for our food, family, and friends. At every meal, we prayed for those who did not have what we had and asked God to help them find what they would need for that day. For parents who are not comfortable with prayer, we suggest that a brief recognition at meals that "our family appreciates what we have and each other" would suffice to build a sense of gratefulness within a child's psyche. Gratefulness is a disposition that brings contentment and allows joy to flourish in a child's life.

When we gather as a family before a meal, we express our gratitude for each other, for what we have to eat, and our intent to care for others and to share our good fortune with them. These basic understandings lead to the values necessary for good citizens, a healthy community, and a happier life.

We hope these personal examples provide you with models that spur your creativity and motivate you to develop your own set of enriched language events for your child's early years. Your stories should reflect your family's history, language, symbols, and faith and celebrate the variety of life in our world.

Your child's personal identity begins to take shape in the stories you share and in the stories you tell about your child. Remember, children are all ears when you speak about them. If you describe your child as clumsy, she will think of herself that way. If you choose to focus on positive aspects of your child in your conversations with other adults about her, she will think positive thoughts about herself too.

Your child will be a member of a global community and you must open the door to your home widely to enable your child to embrace a wide world of opportunities. I would like to close this chapter with this thought that one of our consulting families shared with us:

> Every night we ask our children: What was the best part of your day and what was the worst part of your day? In the first twenty-four months of their lives, we answer for them. After twenty-four months or whenever they can respond, we listen to their answers.

8

The Second and Third Years of a Child's Life

Personal discipline, knowledge, and character are the best friends of successful children. In the second year of a child's life, parents and caregivers begin to teach the language of personal discipline and the virtuous practices that many adults praise in their peers as good character.

Words, phrases, sentences, the logical and illogical, and the inventive and magical stories of early childhood create the underlying principles that color and dress all future feelings of oneself that a child will experience. In a child's second year, as crawling leads to walking, the child begins to test limits that frustrate desire. Parents have to be referees.

Parents need to set limits on a child's explorations that are necessary and reasonable protections of the child's safety. Two-year-olds will challenge those limits. Parents should avoid reacting with anger when a child tests the limits of her world. Parents have to decide what is dangerous and potentially harmful. In one home, it may be climbing onto the keys of the piano. In another home, it may be standing on the top of a toy box or climbing onto the windowsill of the apartment. In every case, a firm "no," an explanation of why the behavior is not safe, and a removal of the child from the danger should suffice. Most often, children will move on to more acceptable behavior if the adult shows them the better option such as pasting stick-to photos in a picture book, coloring in a book with crayons, or building with blocks.

Objects for play should be readily available. Objects *not* for play—like knives and forks—should be safely out of the reach of the child. Two-year-olds try to taste every object they encounter. Tiny toys or parts of toys that a child can swallow are always dangerous.

At two years of age, children learn the difference between "yes" and "no." Parents have to reinforce this difference. Those who let their child ignore a "no" bear the burden of the adolescent who totally ignores the demands and perhaps even the basic laws of society.

Sometimes, a parent's best recourse is to distract a child from a mission to turn the knob on the stove. At other times, a directive "no" is required and movement into another space with several repetitions will be required. Spanking a child should not be an option. Giving a child positive attention to do a positive act produces more positive behavior. A reward for better behavior is available even if it is as simple as a hug. A simple reward is the parent or child caregiver sitting with the child to play a game, even one as simple as rolling a ball.

A "time-out" chair or small rug can serve as a detention center to teach a child limits. Time-out in a child's world can be long if it lasts more than 180 seconds, or three minutes. Parents and caregivers need to set limits; respond to bad behavior with small withdrawals of freedoms and provide tiny rewards for good behavior. A simple response such as a smile accompanied by a loving tone of voice often serves as a large reward for a small child.

Parents and caregivers have to invest their attention in the child during a time-out event. They have to monitor the quiet behavior no matter how brief. After repeated brief losses of freedom to play and crawl, most children learn to live within the limits that parents set.

A cardboard box with cloth toys or other safe toys presents a world for a child to explore. Children find fun in activities such as pulling out things from a box and putting them back in. Naming and describing toys is a wonderful way to involve a child in the discovery of touch, sight and sound, and language forms. Shoeboxes with small toys can serve as discovery centers for three-year-olds and their parents.

Teaching a child to put all of the items back into one box before opening another box is a way to help a child learn to regulate her or his own behavior. A responsible use of toys helps a child build a pattern of care for things outside oneself. Such patterns practiced daily become lifetime disciplines that empower a child to rule over the undisciplined desirous nature that we all share.

Parents have many creative and innovative talents that a child can enjoy and emulate. The fun of parenting expands as parents invent new and interesting ways to share stories, songs or games, and other make-believe events with a child.

Taking a walk in the neighborhood park can be a discovery event for a child who touches her first golden maple leaf in the fall of the year. Many fun animals and birds live in the park. Stories can be told about each of them. Some animals can be given a home in the park even though no one has seen them there. Giraffes, elephants, gorillas, and monkeys can be given names and homes in the park. These make-believe events can lead to terrific conversations with a son or daughter later in the evening before bedtime or at dinner.

One of the board games we played with our children was called Candy Land. The game board had a spinner with numbers that came with the board. The spinner was used to tell each player how many spaces one could move a piece up the circular road toward the Candy Land at the end of the game. By thirty months of age, our children could recognize numbers one to six and count spaces on the board. They enjoyed winning the game and did not like to lose. Most importantly, they learned they did not get what they wanted all of the time; they had to wait for their turn, and sometimes, they had to move backward to go forward.

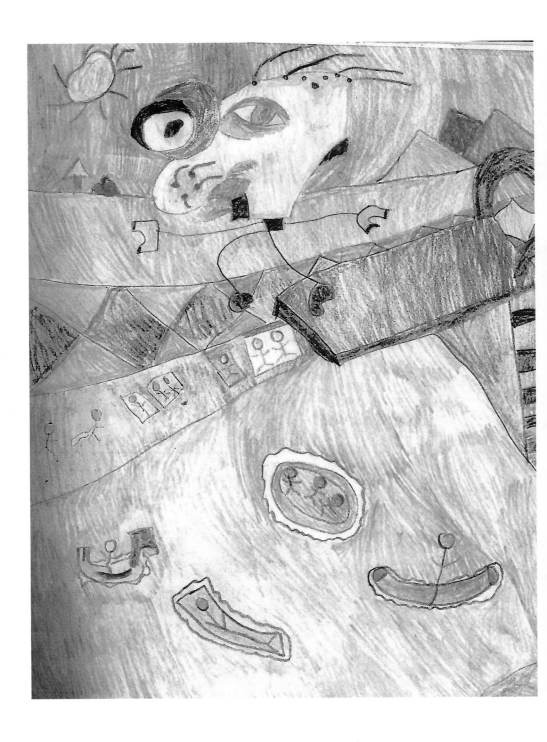

9

Toyland Is Story Land

Naming toys can expand to a game of telling brief stories about each toy. A toy story does not have to be a Disney experience. Think of the fun parents and child can have creating their own stories about toys in a box. Certainly, a mixture of Disney stories and other classic children's stories serve as models for a child's imagination. Parents who engage their child's imagination enable a future of curiosity and inventiveness in their child's life.

A child who is almost three years old can make up stories about toys that interest him or her the most. Parents and adult caregivers can enjoy this creative activity as much as children can. Obviously, children and adults need model stories to use as themes. Most children learn quickly to create variations of an original story theme. They enjoy variations within a familiar story much as jazz musicians enjoy varying from the melody line of a song.

Good stories are available in every culture and language. Often, a child takes great delight in sharing the same story in two or more languages when parents or caregivers have these skills. Parents should have morning stories, daytime stories, and bedtime stories for children.

Wake-up stories should start the day with joyful explorations. Parents can read or tell stories. Small poems or songs make the new day warm and friendly. A song like "Mockin' Bird Hill" with the words, "When the sun in the morning peeps over the hill..." opens the window curtain to a child's day with happy rhythms and fun.

Daytime stories occur just before a nap or just after a nap. Bedtime stories are the very special quiet times when Mom, Dad, or someone special in a child's life takes the time to give unique and undivided attention to one child. Bedtime stories are repeatable favorite stories that a child loves to hear, like the Walt Disney storybook *The Jungle Book: A Friend for Life.*

Stories should stay with a child like old friends. Cherished stories are familiar and predictable. Parents can ask a fifteen- or eighteen-month-old, where is the big star and what does it shine upon? The child can answer a question by pointing to specific events or objects on a page, and in later months the same child can answer with the right words and then with a complete sentence. Long before a child produces words, a child can communicate accurately and judiciously by pointing a finger.

Parents should select new stories one at a time to add to old stories. Children like familiarity and want to have stories repeated. When one reads a story to a child, the child responds to the tone of the parent's voice and to the excitement the parent communicates, and the child's brain maps the sounds and language patterns he or she will use more easily in the future.

By the eighteenth month of a child's life, the child's brain is mapping new sounds and transferring learned sounds to a part of the brain where those sounds stimulate the muscles and vocal cords that the child will use to reproduce the sounds. By listening to repetitive sounds and by reproducing those in appropriate sequences, children gain the ability to reproduce words and to string them into sequential thoughts. All learning is dependent upon the ability of children to recognize patterns and mimic them.

By the end of a child's third year or during the beginning of the fourth year of life, a child should have learned how to respond to three things that are essential for success in school: What "yes" means, what "no" means, and how to wait for a new opportunity.

These three special gifts, plus the capacity to share with others, are learned through practice at home long before one goes to school. Each gift offers a child the power to be successful in a group activity. These powers are transferred, first, from parent to child and then, from the child at home to the child at school. A wise parent practices at home what he or she wants the child to do outside the home.

10

Authentic Care, Help, and Sharing

In the third year of a child's life, other objects and people come to represent a world that the child wants to explore, dominate, understand, and predict. More often than not, a three-year-old is asking "What if . . ." and parents can play this game very effectively by asking the child to predict what might happen next in a story, a poem, a song, or an event that the parent is relating such as "Rain makes puddles that do what?"

Children love to predict what will happen in a story. In *You and Me, Little Bear* by Martin Waddell, Little Bear looks for Big Bear, and what do you think Big Bear is doing after getting done with all of his work? Children begin by giving the right answer: "He is sleeping." Then, they may tease the adult reader by offering a wrong answer such as: "He is eating honey." The adult response— "No, that is not correct"—ends the reading game. Such a response ends the thinking game too. A more enticing response from the adult might be: "Oh, I thought he was playing baseball. Did Martin Waddell, the author, let him play baseball? Let's turn the page and see what Big Bear is doing." This reading game can take many pathways that delight a child.

Developing self-discipline in a child is one of the greatest parental challenges one faces as the child enters her or his third year. Building self-discipline in your child is the most difficult parental behavior to describe. Every child needs to control impulses and desires. Every child needs to become a self-regulating learner, that is, a person who recognizes when she does not know how to do something she wants to do as well as when she or he should or should not do something. A key ingredient of self-regulated learning is a child's capacity to recognize when he needs help to do something and knowing how to ask for that help.

Teaching a child how and when to ask for help is a good beginning. At some point in their explorations, all children reach for something beyond their grasp and an encouraging response to what was spilt or broken helps the child realize that everyone learns from mistakes. When a child spills the contents of a cup, parents extend a gift of confidence by responding: "You can ask for help when something is difficult to reach." When a child says "I can't get this toy to fit in the box," a parent is presented with an opportunity to help the child feel comfortable asking for help. Rather than just doing it for the child, effective parents take the time to explore with the child what the child might do to get the toy to fit better in the box. It could be a simple question such as: "What can we take out of the box to make more room and how can we place both toys back so that they fit?" Through trial and error, the child learns how most adults learn new things.

The child who says "Help me" has taken the first step toward being a self-regulating learner. The parent who does the work for the child has taken a child many steps backward toward dependency and continuous failure. Parents should model the behavior of seeking help. They can respond to the child with a question such as: "Do you think if we empty all of the toys in the box, we can put them back so that they all fit? Let's work together and take turns putting each toy back in the box."

In order for their child to learn something new, such as the name of a flower, a bird, a car, or a vegetable, parents may help the child search for the answer. Parents may guide a child and yet, not do the child's work of discovery. Enabling a child to overcome an obstacle or to find an answer to a question frees the child from dependency and insecurity.

Throughout the third year of a child's life, parents should explore new words, things, and events such as a rainstorm with a child. Where could all that rain come from is a good question. Questions that all parents can explore that children find fun do not have a yes or no for an answer. How does the sun rise? Where does the sun hide at night? What is a cloud? What is a star? How does a paper plane fly?

"Why?" is a favorite question that all children like to ask. Think of all the ways to explore why we mop the floor, why hair changes color, why time marches on. "How?" is another favorite question of children. For instance, a parent might visit the park and ask, "How does a petal of a dandelion feel?"

New parents can have great fun sharing with other recent parents the questions they are exploring with their three-year-olds and especially the responses. The fun depends on the limits of our imaginations. Raising a child is especially fun when parents use their own imaginations to enrich a child's day.

Some things every new parent has to help a three-year-old learn are how to share with others, how to care for someone else, and how to express one's own feelings. Children at this age experience frustrations, anger, and sadness when things do not go their way. Board games such as Candy Land where children have to deal with chance events and face opportunities to lose the game are very healthy developmental experiences for the human psyche. Children acquire a feeling of renewal when they overcome a loss and play the game again. Parents help a child gain a sense of resiliency, drive, and determination as they play games of chance.

During the third year of a child's life, personal discipline and polite and kind behaviors have to be practiced in order for these virtues to become habits. Parents should be more than models of these behaviors. They should be coaches who help their child deal with minor failures, losses, and painful emotions that all humans have to learn to overcome.

One of the greatest gifts a parent can bestow on a child is a sense of gratefulness for the good people and things in her or his life. Gratefulness and feelings of being loved, cherished, and respected as an individual who is different from all other individuals are human dispositions parents can deliver to a child every day.

Holding a child responsible for a few duties in the family home enables the child to become a responsible adult who faces future responsibilities with confidence. Small tasks, such as taking one's own laundry items and placing them in the assigned place, add order and responsibility to a child's world.

All parents who give children duties to perform, no matter how small or insignificant, find that their children seek more responsibility as they grow older. My three brothers-in-law grew up on a dairy farm and as soon as they learned to feed the calves, they wanted to milk the mature cows. When my wife worked with her mother, she wanted to make everything her mother could make, including pies, cakes, and even a skirt and blouse. Children are wonderful in their desire to do and learn more given proper supervision, guidance, and care.

During the period between thirty to forty months of age, many small tasks such as putting shoes or sneakers in a special place, keeping toys organized, putting clothes where they belong, and helping to pick up a room before dinner can be rewarding experiences for the child and the parent.

One day, this responsible child will be driving a car and the early development of personal responsibility will keep her or him much safer than a child who never achieved a sense of personal duty to others.

11

Captain of One's Own Ship

The season of self-regulation begins near the fortieth month of a child's life. Teaching a child to regulate his or her desires, interests, and curiosities does not mean preventing the child from exploring or discovering new identities and talents. To guide a child to acquire personal discipline means helping a child to practice basic virtues or powers that enable careful discoveries.

According to the classical Greek philosopher Aristotle, virtue is a power or discipline acquired through repetitive practice. He believed that the more one practiced a virtue, the more one made the practice a habit. When a person had a virtuous habit, the person was more likely to use the power to repeat the personal discipline in new circumstances. Children who share toys at home share in school.

Highly valued civic virtues seem to be common values across multiple nations and cultures. Some of these virtues are disciplines and powers as I like to call them. They are essential habits that children need to develop at home if they are to thrive in schools, communities, and careers.

Let us explore what these powers might be. One of the parents I interviewed said she wanted her child to be a good person first and then a good student. When I asked her what she meant by a good person, she replied, "I want him to care about how other children feel. I want him to have empathy and be able to feel how someone else might be experiencing a game or even a song. Not everyone can sing on pitch. I want him to empathize with the people around him so that he can relate to others and be part of the larger community later in life."

Alison Gopnik, professor of psychology at University of California, Berkeley, explains that when children play, they explore, do experiments, and investigate causes and effects. She describes children as young as eighteen months old who can distinguish preferences in other people that differ from their own. Her succinct advice to new parents is let children explore with you. In her July 31, 2016, *New York Times* article "What Babies Know," she states, "We don't have to make children learn, we just have to let them learn."

In much the same way, we have to let babies develop personal patience, curiosity, resilience, kindness, and empathy by experiencing these virtues with us. New parents seem motivated by social media and many try to train their babies the way they might train a puppy.

Puppies need love, warmth, and affection just as children do. Puppies will not mimic their owners. They will respond to repeated rewards with repetitive behaviors as all animals do. They will express emotions such as appreciation, care, and concern. Children, on the other hand, have the capacity to acquire unlimited new knowledge, to be selfish or generous, and to imitate what they observe in adults. They require extensive care in their early years. They are "open tablets," in the words of Thomas Aquinas, with enormous capacity for good or its opposite. In spite of some genetic proclivities, children respond to the nurturing and loving care that parents exhibit and tend to seek parental approval from someone who offers them love.

Four-year-olds are great imitators (Berger 2016). They learn best when they imitate others. Often, they mimic exactly what they see and perceive in the actions of their parents and other adult caregivers. Children are motivated to act as others do. Their peers and other adults motivate them to mimic their behaviors in many invisible ways. As Berger notes, all of us are influenced by group behaviors that we witness in others.

Recently, I had the opportunity to speak with a former professional baseball player who spent the last thirty years as a trainer for young athletes. He informed me that he never interfered with a ballplayer in a game. He believed very deeply that an athlete had to learn to correct his or her errors during the game. Practice was a time to perfect a skill. Coaches could be effective models in practice. Games were times for players to use skills, overcome errors, gain confidence, and abandon the fear of failure.

Parents have to choose when to coach and when to let their child explore, practice, make an error, and correct his or her own behavior. An effective coaching technique begins with the question: "Can we try that again?"

Gopnik (2016) noted that the "new information economy, as opposed to the older industrial one, demands more innovation and less imitation, more creativity and less conformity." How does a parent cope with the demands of the global economy for self-motivated learners and avoid the passive parenting practices of the indulgent parent who enables a dependent child?

How does one strike a balance between indulgence and dominance? Walking in the shoes of your child helps you to feel how your child is experiencing the world. How would I feel if I were my son or daughter at this moment? What would I want and need? The answers to these questions offer the direction you should follow. The answers depend on your sensitivity to your child. Sometimes, what your child wants is not what your child needs. Expanding your own empathetic feelings with daily contacts with your four-year-old will provide guidance for your judgments about your child's real needs. Some of the ways that we can expand our empathy for our child's world require us to become a child too.

At first, we observe as a child, quietly. We listen to our child. We watch our child to discover her or his interests. We explore with our child how things work. We play games of chance with our child such as card games and games in which players use a spinner to move across spaces. In such games as checkers, children learn to wait for their turn and they learn they do not always get what they want.

By laughing at the misfortunes of chance and losing spaces, parents teach children how not to be overcome by a loss. Games of physical activity, sports, dance, arts and crafts, playing musical instruments, and singing songs teach children that successful acts require practice. We get to know our child the same way we gain knowledge in any other field: we invest time in learning who our child is.

Another beneficial act is to enjoy outdoor explorations with your child. The mother of the famous Spanish architect and artist, Antoni Gaudi, who designed the Basilica de la Sagrada Familia in Barcelona, took her sickly son on excursions to the countryside to explore how nature designed trees, leaves, and flowers. In those conversations with his mother, the groundwork for his inventive and creative artistry came together. Take delight in conversations and explorations with your child and your child will find delight in you.

Delightful exchanges between parent and child have their own giggle moments. The twinkle in the eye of a parent or grandparent who is playing with a child is a lamp of joy within the soul of both child and playmate. Play holds many joyous moments for those who love one another.

Four-year-olds thrive when they have playmates that like them and care for them. Parents, grandparents, and caregivers can do a great deal to ensure that playmates are kind and good for their young explorer. Watching the playtime and observing interactions provide sufficient information for parents to know how their child is doing. Any interference in children's playtime from a parent should be guided by what is best for all of the children.

A simple set of questions when there is conflict between or among children is: "How can we arrange the play process so that there are more options? If there are only two swings and there are eight children, how do we make a game of swings where everyone has a chance to be pushed on the swing?"

Four-year-olds know when things are fair and when they are not. Fairness is a value that has to be taught and practiced to become a habit among children. One of the great attractions of a democracy is its attempt to use the power of laws to ensure fairness in its society. Democracies depend upon the virtues of their citizens that are learned very early in a child's life.

Effective parents cultivate a sense of fairness in their home and among their children's playmates. Teasing and ridicule are behaviors that these parents do not tolerate as they often turn one child into a target for the other children.

12

Creating a Personal Identity

During the final months before entering school, children recognize as parents do that life is changing. Everyone knows that the school community will be different from home or day care. All of the insecurities within a parent and all of those imbedded within the child surface as a child prepares to go off to school. The locus of control shifts to the school. The child senses quite accurately that she or he does not know how to control and influence those people at school.

At school, a child learns quickly that school people require self-control. Parents have to prepare their child for school by helping the child regulate his or her own desires and emotions. Regulating one's own emotions is not an easy task for some children and definitely a challenge for all children as they enter school.

Self-regulation in school is the management of one's emotions, behaviors, and learning. The first characteristic a child needs to employ at school is good listening skills. Parents can promote good listening skills at home by requiring a child to listen, to follow directions in a game, to take turns with other playmates in a game, and to share toys or food with them.

Listening skills improve as a child repeats parts of a story that a parent reads or tells to the child. Parents who read to children and ask questions about the story prepare their child to formulate a question and to provide answers to questions in the classroom. Simple behaviors at home repeated frequently become school habits that relate to a child's success.

A second characteristic that enables children to learn is the capacity to ask a good question. One element that is very important in forming a question is confidence in one's own capacity to elicit a response from an adult. A strong sense of self-worth that one is worthy of having one's questions answered empowers a child to regulate his or her own learning in school.

Parents engender confidence and self-worth when they treat their child with love, attention, and interest in what the child likes to do or wants to know. A child's sense of self-worth is highly related to the personal attention and love the child receives from parents and other caregivers.

Parents who model good questions for a child about an activity, a story, a film, or a game enable the child to pose good questions. Children enjoy making their own inquiries about many things that interest them, especially when adults share an interest in the question.

Asking questions about a character in a story such as "Why did Christopher Robin become angry with Winnie-the-Pooh?" or "How will Tigger find his way home?"—offers a child opportunities to invent solutions or select the answer from the story. In either case, parents who take delight in their child's response add to their child's sense of self-worth.

A child's sense of self-worth is constructed at home in the first forty-eight months of the child's life. Self-worth and self-identity are similar dispositions that are related to the behaviors and virtues children will practice throughout their adult lives. When parents tell stories about their child, the child hears and learns if she or he is good, helpful, valuable, and loved.

Many children take a long time beyond forty-eight months to gain a sense of self-worth and self-identity. In adolescence, as a teenager, your child's dispositions will be challenged again. The challenges keep coming all through life. As a new parent, your job is to establish a strong foundation of personal identity. Trust your child to build his or her own world on the foundation that you construct together in your child's earliest years.

The teenage years, higher education, and the world of work have their own challenges that your child will face as best he or she can with the foundation of values and personal strength you helped to construct with your child. Act so that you can feel that you have done your best to love and support your child as an individual and to trust your child to recover from bad choices. We all make some bad choices and have to retrace our options and select a better choice more in line with our family values. The best golfers are those who can recover from errors and learn not to repeat them. Effective parents and successful children learn from their errors and avoid repeating them.

Parents can help children gain the skills that will enable them to continuously improve by asking, "What could you have done differently?" We have heard the saying "the apple does not fall far from the tree." Parents are the first models that a child imitates. Parents teach their child their own values, interests, and skills in many invisible ways (Berger 2016). Parents can teach in a haphazard way without much forethought or parents can make choices about how they will deal with their child. They can anticipate how they want their child to feel, to behave, and to enjoy life. They can plan to have events that support their child's development as an individual with self-control or they can let events take their course and conduct a game of chance in raising their child.

As their child grows, parents face choices about their own behavior and practices. Parents have to practice with their child what they hope their child will be able to do, to feel and to enjoy. When one of our sons was six years old, he spent a year taking my hand and bringing me to the television when an antismoking ad came on the television. He kept asking me to stop smoking. Fortunately for me, he succeeded in his quest to have me quit smoking.

One of our consulting families has a plaque hanging in their home hallway with sixteen family rules. I asked the children to tell me the ten rules they think every family should have. Their list follows:

Love each other

Respect one another

Keep your promises

Say I love you

Do your best

Laugh at yourself

Dream big

Be grateful

Be happy

Hug often

Parenting is an awesome and complex vocation. Raising a child is a sacred gift. As the Judeo-Christian Bible states: "We are all created in the image and likeness of God." We are born into the fourth dimension and encapsulated within a brief period of time. According to this Holy Book and many other religious sacred texts, our purpose as human beings is to reflect God's love, mercy, and forgiveness. If God is truth and love, then we are created to love one another. Parents who give their children love, mercy, kindness, and attention discover in their old age that their children acquired these virtues and return them as gifts to their elderly parents.

May you, Dear Reader, be so fortunate as to have children who respect and love you. Please keep precious your presence in your child's life by enjoying playtime, chore time, and spiritual time with your child.

References

Aquinas, T. 1948. *Summa Theologia*. New York: Benziger Brothers.

Aristotle. 1984. *The Complete Works of Aristotle*. Edited by J. Barnes. Princeton, New Jersey: Princeton University Press.

Berger, J. 2016. *Invisible Influence*. New York: Social Dynamics Group, Simon & Schuster.

Gerald, I. 2007. "A Case Study of School-Related Parenting Practices, Parental Styles and Achievement in an Urban Elementary School." Unpublished dissertation. Dowling College, UMI Proquest.

Gopnik, A. July 31, 2016. "What Babies Know." *New York Times*.

Hart, B. and Risley, T. 1995. *Meaningful Differences in the Everyday Experience of Young American Children*. Baltimore, Maryland: Paul H. Brooks Publishing.

Jeter, D. May 14, 2017. *New York Times*.

Judeo-Christian Bible. 1950. New York: Alba House: Benziger Brothers Publishing.

Kellogg, S. 1973. *The Island of the Skog*. New York: Dial Publishing.

Lesaux, N.K. and Kieffer, M.J. September 2010. "Exploring Sources of Reading Comprehension Difficulties Among Language Minority Learners and Their Classmates in Early Adolescence." *American Educational Research Journal*, V. 47, No.3, pp 596–632.

Marsoli, L. A. 1998. *Walt Disney's The Jungle Book: A Friend for Life*. Disney Enterprises.

National Reading Panel. 2000. *Teaching Children to Read*. Washington District of Columbia: National Institute of Child Health and Human Development.

Rotello, C. September/October 2005. "When Your Kid Whines, Screams, Hits, Kicks and Bites—Relax." *Yale Alumni Magazine*.

Sandburg, C. 1998. *Grassroots* (compilation of poems). Illustrations by Wendell Minor. New York: Harcourt Brace and Company.

Scarry, R. 1994. *Best Balloon Ride Ever!* New York: Golden Books.

Shaw, M. 1941. *Walt Disney's Bambi*. Original story by Felix Salten. Racine, Wisconsin: Western Publishing Company.

Simonee, S. 2013. "An Analysis of How Multicultural Adult Orphans Achieve Economic Success." Unpublished dissertation. Dowling College, UMI-Proquest.

Waddell, M. 1996. *You and Me, Little Bear*. Cambridge, Massachusetts: Candlewick Press.

Yeats, W. B. 1994. *The Collected Poems of W. B. Yeats*. Hertfordshire, England: Wordsworth Editions Limited.

Appendix

Model songs and stories to share with your baby

Songs

Do-Re-Mi (from *The Sound of Music*)

Happy Birthday

Hush, Little Baby

Toora, Loora, Loora

Twinkle, Twinkle, Little Star

Books

Chipmunk Song

Guess How Much I Love You

Goldilocks and the Three Bears

I Loved You Before You Were Born

Jack and the Beanstalk

The Last Star at Night

The Jungle Book A Friend for Life

Winnie the Pooh's Valentine

About the Author

Robert J. Manley, PhD is a former superintendent of schools at West Babylon Public Schools in New York. He is a retired professor of educational leadership at Dowling College. Currently, he is editor-in-chief of the *Journal for Leadership and Instruction* published by SCOPE Educational Services, Smithtown, New York. He is the coauthor with Richard J. Hawkins of *Designing School Systems for All Students: A Toolbox to Fix America's Schools* and *Making the Common Core Standards Work: Using Professional Development to Build World-Class Schools*.

About the Illustrator

Norah E. Manley studies graphic design at Bergen Community College in New Jersey. She has overcome many challenges during her years in schools. At the beginning of each chapter in this book, Norah presents a fresh view of the primary theme she found in this section of the book. Her vision of how a child experiences those parenting behaviors and dispositions in each chapter offers new parents guidance for them to celebrate their child's unique creativity.